Humanitarian Organisations

Doctors Without Borders

Médecins Sans Frontières

Ann Parry

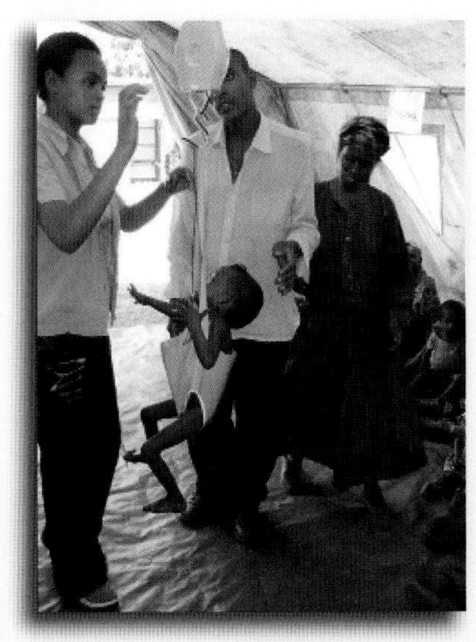

MACMILLAN
LIBRARY

For Jack and Win Parry—exceptional and loving parents.

First published in 2005 by
MACMILLAN EDUCATION AUSTRALIA PTY LTD
627 Chapel Street, South Yarra 3141

Visit our website at www.macmillan.com.au

Associated companies and representatives throughout the world.

National Library of Australia
Cataloguing-in-Publication data

Parry, Ann, 1949–.
Doctors without borders.

Includes index.
For upper primary school students.
ISBN 0 7329 9738 0.

1. Médecins sans frontières (Association) – Juvenile literature.
I. Title. (Series: Parry, Ann, 1949– Humanitarian organisations).

610.6

Edited by Angelique Campbell-Muir and Anna Fern
Cover and text design by Raul Diche
Maps by Pat Kermode
Photo research by Jes Senbergs

Printed in China

Acknowledgements
The author and the publisher are grateful to the following for permission to reproduce copyright material:

Cover photographs: Doctors without Borders volunteers in Iran, courtesy of Tim Dirven. Child health centre in Africa, courtesy of Kurt Tonini/MSF. Doctors without Borders volunteers in Peru, courtesy of Bruno De Cock/MSF.

Amnesty International, p. 4 (logo); Australian Red Cross, p. 4 (logo); Australian Volunteers International, p. 4 (logo); Peter Boer, p. 30 (right); Corbis, pp. 6, 9; Henry Debussman, p. 28; Tim Dirven, pp. 10, 15; Doctors Without Borders/ Médecins Sans Frontières (MSF), pp. 4 (logo), 5; Greenpeace, p. 4 (logo); Marina Khachukaeva, pp. 22, 23; Arie Kievit, p. 17; Janet Komba, p. 26; Claude Mahoudeau, p. 19; Robert Maletta, p. 16; MSF, p. 30 (left); Bruno De Cock/MSF, p. 29; Michael Neuman/MSF, p. 27; Kurt Tonini/MSF, pp. 1, 14, 18, 20; Linda Van Weyenberg/MSF, p. 11; Sally Murray, p. 24; Espen Rasmussen, p. 21; Save the Children, p. 4 (logo); Juan Carlos Tomasi, pp. 7, 25; United Nations, p. 8.

While every care has been taken to trace and acknowledge copyright, the publisher tenders their apologies for any accidental infringement where copyright has proved untraceable. Where the attempt has been unsuccessful, the publisher welcomes information that would redress the situation.

Please note
At the time of printing, the Internet addresses appearing in this book were correct. Owing to the dynamic nature of the Internet, however, we cannot guarantee that all these addresses will remain correct.

Contents

What is a humanitarian organisation? 4
About Doctors Without Borders 5
History of Doctors Without Borders 6
The founders of Doctors Without Borders 8
Early work 9
Core values of Doctors Without Borders 10
How Doctors Without Borders works 11
Where in the world is Doctors Without Borders? 12
Timeline 13

Concerns, campaigns and classic actions 14
- Natural disasters 14
- Wars and conflicts 16
- Epidemics 18
- Lack of access to health care 20

The people of Doctors Without Borders 22
- MARINA KHACHUKAEVA Program coordinator 22
- SALLY MURRAY Doctor 24
- JANET KOMBA Midwife 26
- HENRY DEBUSSMAN Logistician 28

What can you do? 30
Glossary 31
Index 32

Glossary words

When a word is printed in **bold**, its meaning is included on that page. You can also look up its meaning in the Glossary on page 31.

What is a humanitarian organisation?

Humanitarian organisations work to help solve problems in countries around the world, wherever there is a need for their help. They are sometimes called aid agencies, not-for-profit or non-government organisations (NGOs). Some organisations, such as Greenpeace, work to protect the environment. Others, such as Amnesty International and the International Red Cross, work to protect people's **human rights** or provide for their basic needs in times of conflict and disaster. Doctors Without Borders sends **volunteers** anywhere in the world to give medical help to people affected by disasters. Groups like Save the Children and Australian Volunteers International help rebuild communities that need food, education and advice.

Some humanitarian organisations are given money by governments to help run their programs. They also work hard to collect enough money from the public to keep going. Some of their workers are volunteers and are not paid, while others work for a small wage.

The *Humanitarian Organisations* series focusses on six well-known organisations and explains how they help those in need around the world.

Glossary words

humanitarian
devoted to people's welfare and the promotion of social reform

human rights
a set of rights, such as the right to a fair trial, laid down by the United Nations

volunteers
people who donate their time to a cause

australianvolunteers international

Australian Volunteers International

The Red Cross

Greenpeace

Save the Children

Amnesty International

Doctors Without Borders

About Doctors Without Borders

Doctors Without Borders, also known as Médecins Sans Frontières, delivers emergency medical aid all over the world. The organisation has no connections with governments or political groups, and does not work for profit. Every year, about 3000 volunteer doctors, nurses and support staff work in trouble spots around the world helping people living in crisis situations.

Volunteers

Many of the volunteers see awful scenes every day. Some volunteer for a fixed period of time. Others have decided to make humanitarian aid work an ongoing part of their lives.

Doctors Without Borders teams are currently in 78 countries, working with more than 15 000 locally recruited staff. They work in conditions that are always challenging, and sometimes dangerous.

Doctors Without Borders volunteers provide relief after natural disasters, help casualties of war and run emergency feeding centres during **famines**. They fight disease and organise mass **vaccination** programs to prevent **epidemics** from spreading.

Long-term health projects

Doctors Without Borders also has longer-term health projects. These projects can help people such as refugees, street children or people who may have no access to treatment because they live in isolated or **disadvantaged** communities. Volunteers also help to train local medical staff, provide safe drinking water and **sanitation** facilities, and help to rebuild hospitals.

Main goal

Wherever the teams are working, their goal is always the same: to provide essential medical aid to those who need it most, without **discrimination**.

Did you know?

An average of 3000 Doctors Without Borders volunteers are at work in the field each year.

Glossary words

famines
times when food is extremely scarce and people are starving

vaccination
medicine given to protect against infectious diseases

epidemics
diseases that spread rapidly throughout a community

disadvantaged
having a difficulty in some area, such as health, income or education, which prevents the person from leading a full life

sanitation
drainage and disposal of sewage

discrimination
unfair treatment because of race, religion or other unjust reason

This is the logo for Doctors Without Borders.

History of Doctors Without Borders

Doctors Without Borders began in 1971 when two groups of international medical relief doctors began talking about their desire to help save more lives. Some of the doctors had been helping victims of a **civil war** in Biafra (presently part of Nigeria), in Africa. They had come to believe that restrictions put in place by governments were preventing medical aid from getting through. They decided to form a group that would be able to provide help more effectively.

More effective help

Until this time, the International Red Cross and various military forces had been in charge of most medical treatment in disaster areas. Red Cross workers, though, were not allowed to speak out about abuses they had witnessed. They also had to obtain permission from both sides in a conflict before they were allowed to work in any country.

With wars increasing around the world, many more civilians were also suffering. The French doctors who had worked in Biafra knew that many people had died because aid organisations could not reach them. They promised themselves that next time they would be ready to save many more lives. Two smaller French medical aid groups then joined together and became Doctors Without Borders.

Did you know?

The French Red Cross sent 50 volunteer doctors to Biafra between 1968 and 1970.

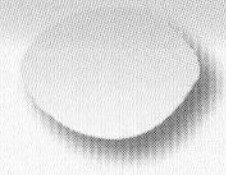

Glossary word

civil war
war between different groups within a country

Many civilians, such as these women and children in Biafra, in 1969, face illness and starvation as a result of war.

Starting small

In the early years, Doctors Without Borders remained a small organisation. It was made up entirely of volunteers who held other jobs as well. The organisation had little money, and did not ask for donations. There was not enough experience for the group to work on its own. After 1976, things began to change. Doctors Without Borders went to work in a war zone in Lebanon. A year later it was offered a free advertising campaign which helped people think of it as an aid organisation that worked in dangerous emergencies.

Main area of work

From 1978, the huge growth in refugee camps all over the world gave Doctors Without Borders its main area of work. This work continues today. Some things have changed, though. Fundraising now brings in enough money to support the work. Doctors Without Borders doctors make more public statements about the things they have witnessed and more international teams are formed for missions. Medical staff with satellite phones and full medical kits now arrive within days of a disaster report.

This mobile health clinic visits people who live in remote parts of Colombia, in South America, who may not have seen a doctor in years.

Did you know?

Doctors Without Borders has four logistical centres based in Europe and East Africa, and stocks of emergency materials are stored in Central America and East Asia. This ensures that, within 24 hours, planes can be loaded with essential equipment and flown into a crisis area anywhere in the world.

The founders of Doctors Without Borders

Doctors Without Borders was not founded by any one person. It developed from the actions of a group of 13 concerned people, including doctors and journalists. Some of these were doctors who had provided medical aid for people caught up in the war in Biafra in the 1960s. Through this experience, they saw a need for a new organisation to be created that could have greater independence from government control to provide help whenever it was needed. At the same time, another group of doctors who had volunteered to go and help the victims of a tidal wave in Bangladesh also became interested in forming an emergency medical aid group.

Two groups become one

In 1970, the Emergency Medical and Surgical Intervention Group was formed, followed by another group called French Medical Relief. Many doctors responded and volunteered for overseas work. In 1971, these two volunteer groups joined together to become Doctors Without Borders.

These Bangladeshi people's homes were destroyed in a cyclone in 1973.

Did you know?

About 200 000 people were killed by the cyclone-driven tidal wave that hit Bangladesh in 1970. Over 100 000 people were declared missing.

Early work

For the first five years, Doctors Without Borders was a small group, working wherever their time and finances would allow.

First mission

Their first independent mission was to Nicaragua in 1972. Nicaragua is a poor country in Central America whose capital city, Managua, was devastated by a severe earthquake in 1972. The entire centre of the city, including two of the three main hospitals, was destroyed. The destruction and chaos was so bad that much of the aid sent from other countries was not getting through to the victims. Doctors Without Borders believed that their way of working would make a difference.

Dealing with typhoid

The most immediate problem was a likely outbreak of a disease called typhoid. Typhoid spreads where there is no clean water or sanitation. Doctors Without Borders volunteers helped to bury bodies and treat the sick, as well as trying to re-establish proper water supplies.

Because of the lack of resources and experience, this early mission did not work very well. In this instance, American assistance had arrived well ahead of Doctors Without Borders. Today, the work of Doctors Without Borders is very different.

The Nicaraguan capital Managua was destroyed by an earthquake in 1972.

Up to 100 000 people were killed and 300 000 people lost their homes in the Nicaraguan earthquake.

Core values of Doctors Without Borders

Core values are the things that a person, group or organisation really believes in. The values are used to work out rules of behaviour. Doctors Without Borders has four core values, which it sometimes calls main principles, that are followed by all their workers.

Help without discrimination

Doctors Without Borders helps people who are suffering. They might be victims of natural or human-made disasters, or they may have been caught up in wars or fighting. Doctors Without Borders helps anyone in need, whatever race, religion, belief system or political group they may belong to.

Neutrality

Doctors Without Borders is strictly **neutral** and does not take sides. It is only concerned with bringing medical help to those who need it, and insists that its doctors and health staff have complete freedom to carry out their work.

Ethics

Doctors Without Borders volunteers promise to follow standard medical codes of **ethics** and not to get involved in any particular groups connected with countries that they are helping.

No compensation

Doctors Without Borders' work is dangerous. Volunteers have no right to **compensation** for themselves or their families other than what the organisation can afford.

An Iranian family is helped by Doctors Without Borders after their home was destroyed by an earthquake in 2004.

Did you know?

In August 2003, the **United Nations** Security Council passed a resolution on the need to protect humanitarian workers.

Glossary words

neutral
not taking either side in an argument or fight

United Nations
an organisation made up of representatives from many countries, which deals with international peace and security

ethics
personal rules and standards of behaviour

compensation
money paid for injury or suffering

How Doctors Without Borders works

Doctors Without Borders is a private international humanitarian organisation, with separate branches in many countries. Most of its members are doctors and health workers, but many others also contribute to the work. Teams are made up of people with qualifications in medicine, nursing, **logistics**, engineering and administration.

There are two main areas of activity for Doctors Without Borders:

- quick help in emergencies, such as during a natural disaster or conflict
- longer-term health care programs for people affected by diseases such as **tuberculosis** or **HIV/AIDS**.

Independence

The most important thing about Doctors Without Borders is that it is independent. Three-quarters of its money comes from private donations. It limits the amount of money it accepts from any government or international bodies such as the European Union.

The reason for this is that it allows Doctors Without Borders to make its own decisions about who it will help, and how it will run an emergency intervention.

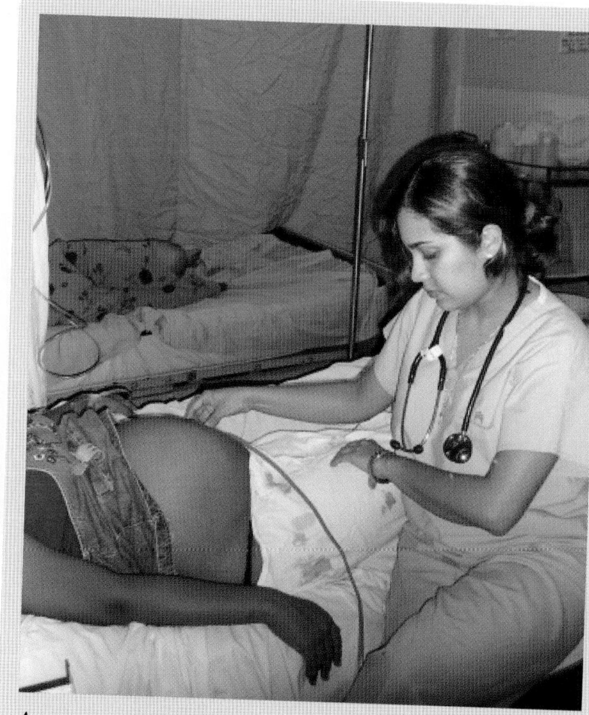

A pregnant woman in Nicaragua receives emergency medical help.

Speaking out

In some circumstances, the teams may come across atrocities or witness the exclusion of people from health care. In these cases, members can speak out and call upon governments, warring parties and international bodies to take responsible action.

Glossary words

logistics
organisation of people, equipment and procedures to get a job done

tuberculosis
an infectious disease where lumps form in parts of the body such as the lungs and bones, and cause those parts to break down

HIV/AIDS
a virus that stops the body from fighting against infections

Where in the world is Doctors Without Borders?

Doctors Without Borders works in many countries around the world. This map shows where major Doctors Without Borders campaigns are located.

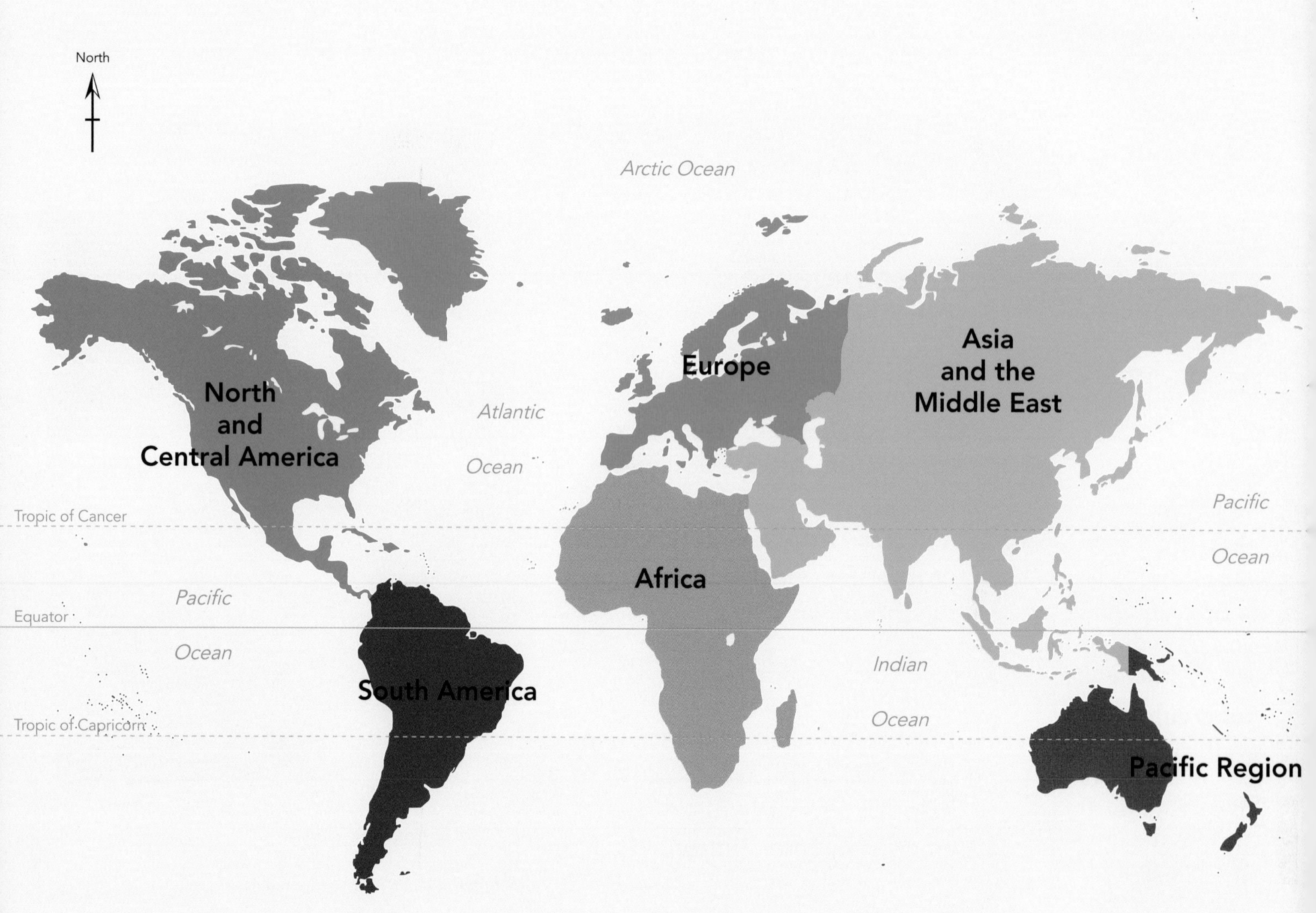

Key to countries

ASIA AND THE MIDDLE EAST
Afghanistan, Azerbaijan, Bangladesh, Burma, Cambodia, China, East Timor, India, Indonesia, Iran, Iraq, Kazakhstan, Kyrgyzstan, Laos, Lebanon, Mongolia, North Korea, Pakistan, Palestinian Authority, Papua New Guinea, Philippines, Sri Lanka, Tajikistan, Thailand, Turkmenistan, Uzbekistan, Vietnam, Yemen

EUROPE
Albania, Armenia, Belgium, Bosnia–Herzegovina, Bulgaria, Chechnya, France, Georgia, Ingushetia, Italy, Kosovo, Luxembourg, Macedonia, Romania, Russian Federation, Spain, Ukraine

PACIFIC REGION
None

AFRICA
Algeria, Angola, Benin, Burkina Faso, Burundi, Central African Republic, Chad, Congo, Côte d'Ivoire, Egypt, Equatorial Guinea, Eritrea, Ethiopia, Guinea, Guinea-Bissau, Kenya, Liberia, Madagascar, Malawi, Mali, Mauritania, Mozambique, Nigeria, Rwanda, Sierra Leone, Somalia, South Africa, Sudan, Tanzania, Uganda, Zambia

NORTH AND CENTRAL AMERICA
Belize, Costa Rica, Cuba, El Salvador, Guatemala, Haiti, Honduras, Mexico, Nicaragua, Panama

SOUTH AMERICA
Bolivia, Brazil, Colombia, Ecuador, Nicaragua, Peru, Venezuela

Timeline

Doctors Without Borders has been working to help people since it began in 1971.

1971	Doctors Without Borders is founded by a group of French doctors and journalists after the famine in Biafra, Nigeria. First natural disaster response is undertaken, in Nicaragua. First large-scale intervention to a refugee crisis is undertaken, in Cambodia.
1976	Doctors Without Borders attempts its first major intervention into a war zone, in Lebanon. Programs to fight malnutrition are launched as a response to the famine in Ethiopia.
1986	Doctors Without Borders expands into Europe.
1995	Doctors Without Borders offers aid to civilians in Chechnya (near the Caspian Sea) and to people in refugee camps in neighbouring countries.
1996	The Doctors Without Borders network grows significantly. The Norway section is founded, joining partner sections in Italy, the United States of America, Canada, the United Kingdom, Denmark, Hong Kong, Japan, Sweden, Greece, Germany, Australia and Austria.
1999	Doctors Without Borders launches its campaign for access to essential medicines.
2000	Asylum seekers (many from north and west Africa) flee to Europe. Programs assisting asylum seekers and undocumented immigrants in France, Italy, Spain and Belgium are expanded.
2001	The HIV/AIDS pandemic (when a disease spreads through a country or around the world)—Doctors Without Borders starts providing special therapy that lengthens the lives of people living with AIDS in seven countries.
2003	The United States of America invades Iraq. Doctors Without Borders teams remain in Baghdad during the war and challenge the United States government on its failure to provide adequate medical care to civilians. Doctors Without Borders opens a free clinic for HIV/AIDS patients in Xiangfan, China.
2004	Doctors Without Borders works desperately to save villages affected by fighting in Sudan. They treat more than 12 000 malnourished children in feeding centres, and treat people suffering from diarrhoea, malaria, respiratory infections and hepatitis E.

Concerns, campaigns and classic actions

Doctors Without Borders is concerned about a range of problems throughout the world. It identifies specific campaigns and takes action accordingly.

CONCERNS

Natural disasters

Doctors Without Borders is concerned about the effects of natural disasters. Natural disasters include earthquakes, floods and droughts. In **underdeveloped countries**, natural disasters can often lead to outbreaks of disease and many deaths after the immediate crisis has passed. Doctors Without Borders aims to deliver the most rapid and effective aid possible before the problems become even more widespread.

CAMPAIGNS

One of the great strengths of Doctors Without Borders is its logistics. In a disaster situation logistics are critical. Help must arrive quickly for a variety of problems. A mobile hospital might be needed to treat the injured, or a feeding centre set up in a famine area. The feeding centre may need to continue after the immediate danger of starvation has passed, to improve people's health, particularly in the case of children.

After a flood or earthquake, clinics may be needed to vaccinate the population against diseases such as **cholera**, which can break out when water and sanitation systems are destroyed. These systems will also need to be rebuilt as soon as possible to prevent further epidemics. Shelter will need to be provided for the sick.

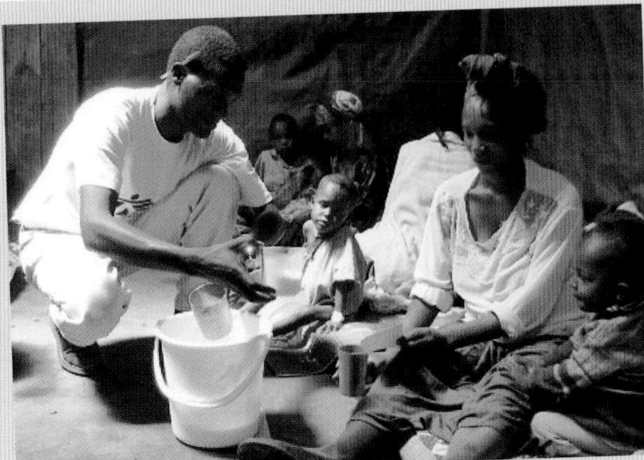

A Doctors Without Borders team member distributes food to improve the health of these children.

Glossary words

underdeveloped countries
countries that are not able to provide a good standard of living for their citizens in such areas as health, education and housing

cholera
infectious and often fatal diarrhoea, spread by poor sanitation

Each disaster is different and each presents different problems. Doctors Without Borders now has a set of plans and systems that it uses to give the best results. These plans and systems must be standard enough so that workers can put them into operation smoothly. They also must be flexible enough to adjust to each new situation.

Doctors Without Borders also tries to prevent the development of new disasters by running surveillance programs. This means that it has workers in areas that are at a higher risk of suffering from the effects of floods, earthquakes and famines. These workers pay close attention to what is happening. This can allow Doctors Without Borders to take early action.

Classic action

After a terrible earthquake in Iran in 2003, Doctors Without Borders immediately sent in a team to asses the situation, including doctors and first-aid equipment. Tonnes of medical and emergency supplies as well as water-treatment equipment were flown in from France and other countries. Other medical teams also set out from Belgium and Spain. At first there was not even water or electricity available to help the wounded. Gradually the doctors were able to make some progress, but a great deal of on-going help will still be needed.

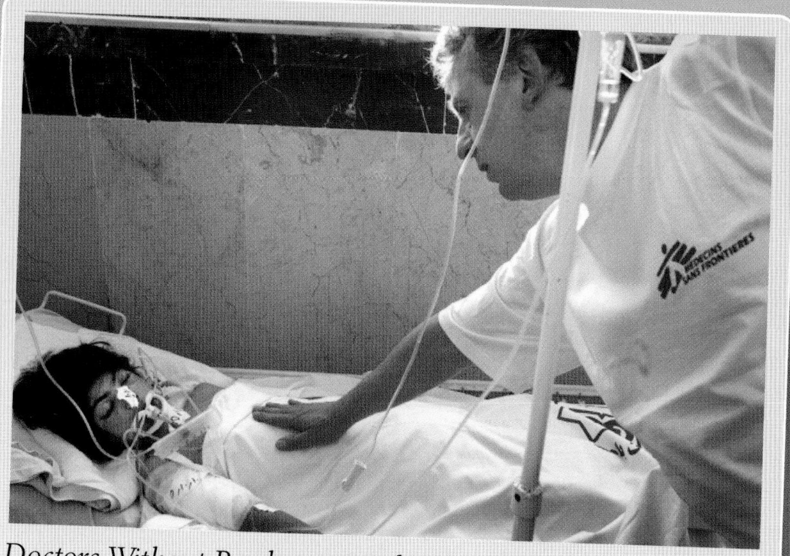

Doctors Without Borders treated many patients after the 2003 Iranian earthquake.

CONCERNS

Wars and conflicts

Doctors Without Borders is concerned that every day, in some part of the world, fighting is going on. It could be a war between countries, or between groups within a country. Doctors Without Borders provides medical care for the wounded and sick, who may have no other help available.

CAMPAIGNS

Doctors Without Borders is often the first organisation to arrive in a conflict zone. Its volunteers sometimes work alone in dangerous and uncomfortable situations. They bring with them hospital kits with enough drugs and equipment to set up and run a 30-bed hospital and clinic for three months. These kits are pre-packaged so that they can be loaded, transported and delivered to wherever they are needed quickly and easily.

Doctors Without Borders never takes sides in a war or fighting. It insists that all hospitals, medical staff and patients are regarded as absolutely neutral. Anyone carrying arms is banned. Doctors Without Borders operates on the wounded, saving lives and repairing damaged limbs. Volunteers sometimes need to remain in a country for years after the actual fighting has stopped, to help with long-term recovery programs for mental and physical health.

Doctors Without Borders staff fly in supplies to the war-torn country of Sudan, in 1998.

CAMPAIGNS

Conflicts today are having much more serious effects on civilian populations. Wars have always had horrible impacts on innocent victims of the fighting, but most combatants avoided this wherever possible. Modern wars seem to be different, with women and children being killed and injured in ever-increasing numbers. Doctors Without Borders tries to provide an area where civilians can be looked after and protected. Its volunteers work in any sort of conditions to show the local population that they have not been abandoned, and that someone cares about them. This is an important feature of the organisation's work.

Classic action

In the early 1990s war broke out in what was then called Yugoslavia in Europe. The entire population experienced situations of horror and **trauma**. Throughout this war, Doctors Without Borders ran surgery programs, distributed medical supplies and drugs to hospitals and clinics, operated mobile clinics and worked in refugee camps. After the war they set up mental health programs to help people recover from the awful things they had suffered. These programs continued for many years.

Patients receive medical help from a Doctors Without Borders mobile clinic in the former Yugoslavia.

Glossary word

trauma
emotional shock

CONCERNS

Epidemics

Doctors Without Borders is concerned that more people die today from infectious diseases than from any other cause. Severe outbreaks of disease are called epidemics. Epidemics must be responded to quickly. The sick must be treated to prevent the disease from spreading to those who are still healthy.

CAMPAIGNS

Cholera, **malaria** and measles are examples of dangerous infectious diseases. They can kill up to 24 000 people a day in an underdeveloped country. Doctors Without Borders runs a two-part program to tackle these sorts of infectious diseases.

Firstly, Doctors Without Borders sets up programs to treat the sick. It has medical teams on stand-by for this work. When an epidemic breaks out, both hospitals and outpatient clinics can be quickly set up, and life saving drugs supplied. This saves many lives, but many patients still die.

Secondly, Doctors Without Borders operates programs that try to prevent epidemics from starting at all. Disease prevention starts with knowing more about the topic. Doctors Without Borders uses special testing kits to find out exactly what its volunteers will be dealing with in a given situation. They also need to know where the disease is coming from and how it is spreading.

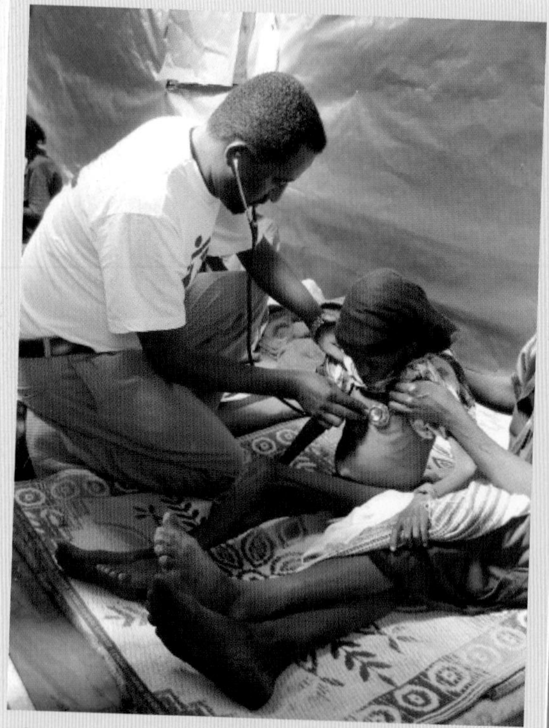

This Ethiopian child is being treated at a Doctors Without Borders intensive-care unit.

Glossary word

malaria
a fever spread by mosquitoes

CAMPAIGNS

Once information about a disease that could become an epidemic has been collected, a prevention program can be started. For measles, mass vaccinations will be needed. For cholera, clean drinking water and proper sanitation systems are the answer. Mosquito nets for beds and education will help to prevent malaria. Doctors Without Borders is involved in all of these actions.

What makes disease prevention so difficult in poorer countries is that the effective treatments can be far too expensive, or can stop working after a time. Doctors Without Borders campaigns for research into new drug treatments, and also for the provision of cheap, effective medicines for all patients who need them.

Classic action

The people of Mozambique, Africa, suffer particularly from cholera. They have more epidemics with a higher death rate. Until now, the government has only been able to respond to epidemics, rather than stop them from happening. Treating an epidemic is expensive and strains the health system. Doctors Without Borders is working on a new vaccination program to supplement better water and sanitation systems. In 2002 it used a new vaccine to treat approximately 50 000 people and assessed its effectiveness.

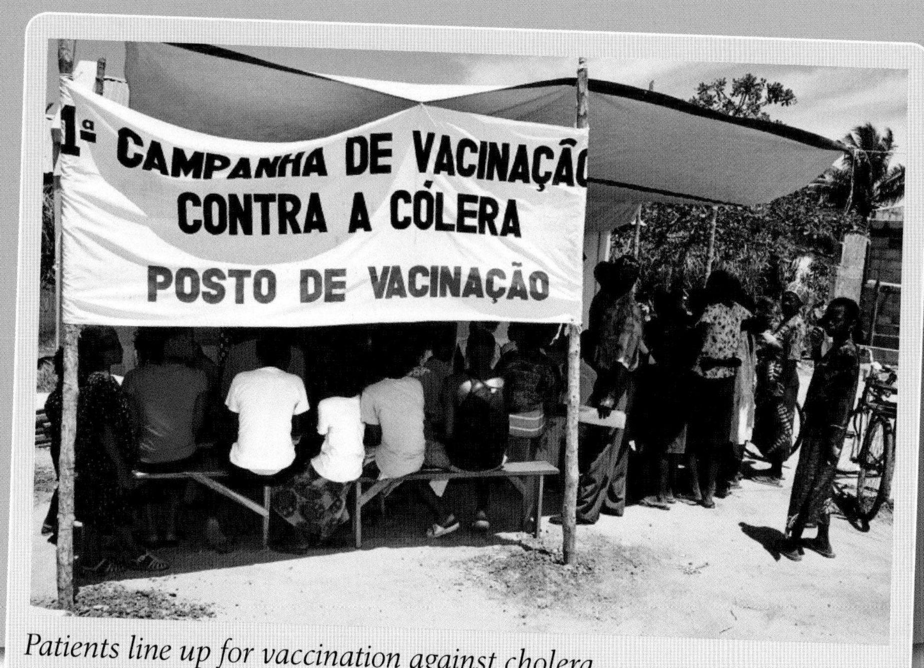

Patients line up for vaccination against cholera.

CONCERNS

Lack of access to health care

Doctors Without Borders is concerned that in many countries around the world, general health is poor. Governments do not provide good enough medical services, and death rates are much higher than in wealthier countries. Some areas have no real health care at all. Women and children can be particularly at risk.

CAMPAIGNS

Doctors Without Borders provides health care in many countries where there are not enough medical facilities, or where there are no medical facilities at all. Volunteers help to re-establish hospitals and clinics for people who need treatment. They also help to build better water supplies and toilet facilities, to lessen the chances of diseases like **dysentery** and cholera taking hold in the community.

They can help to train local medical and paramedical workers, such as nurses and medical scientists, to run the health programs. Volunteers may also work alongside local doctors and nurses in already existing hospitals to provide specialist health care support, for example, for women who are having babies.

Child health centres like this one, in Africa, help to prevent disease and malnutrition.

Glossary word

dysentery
a disease where the intestine becomes inflamed, which causes diarrhoea

Doctors Without Borders also involves itself in some longer-term projects. It helps groups who are disadvantaged, such as street children, prisoners, refugees and those living in remote areas.

Doctors Without Borders also provides medical care for people living with diseases such as malaria, tuberculosis and HIV/AIDS. Diseases like HIV/AIDS are very expensive to treat. There are millions of people throughout the world who cannot afford to buy the drugs they need to prolong their lives. Doctors Without Borders provides treatment, counselling and health education to communities affected by HIV/AIDS.

Classic action

Doctors Without Borders first arrived in Cambodia, South-East Asia, in 1989. Over one million people had been killed as a result of internal fighting and a government policy of killing educated people in favour of 'simple farmers'. Very few doctors survived and medical care in Cambodia was almost non-existent. Doctors Without Borders has helped to rebuild the health system, research effective malaria treatments, provide medicine for sufferers of HIV/AIDS and set up a clinic for people suffering from long-term illness.

Cambodian patients receive medicines at a Doctors Without Borders pharmacy.

The people of Doctors Without Borders

Doctors Without Borders helps people and communities all over the world. Here are four volunteers who use their own specialised skills to help in different situations.

MARINA KHACHUKAEVA Progam coordinator

Marina Khachukaeva believes that ignoring people's suffering can only make the world worse.

Marina Khachukaeva joined Doctors Without Borders in 1995 when the war began between the Chechen Republic and Russia. She was part of the team of local staff. She began work as a translator, and now works as a coordinator of a program to help people displaced by the fighting.

The war was extremely difficult for the whole Chechen nation. Cities and villages were destroyed and no one was safe. People felt frustrated and unable to defend themselves or help each other. Marina was feeling completely desperate when Doctors Without Borders approached her and asked her to do humanitarian work for people in need. The chance to make positive changes for people in need gave Marina a new will to live and hope for the future.

But Marina's work for Doctors Without Borders is not always positive. There are moments of frustration when she suffers deeply from what she sees, and from her inability to stop the unjust things from happening. Doctors Without Borders cannot always change the world, but it tries to improve it by helping people to survive.

Did you know?

Marina works in a country called Ingushetia. It borders Chechnya, near the Caspian Sea.

Marina helps to distribute tents to people whose homes in Ingushetia have been destroyed.

Marina has seen some terrible things while doing active work in the field. In 1996 she visited a village called Samashki that had been completely destroyed by the army. Entry was forbidden. Doctors Without Borders was one of the first organisations to enter, and its volunteers found a truly shocking scene. The buildings were still burning. Bodies of villagers and their farm animals lay everywhere. It was deathly quiet. Finally, some survivors began creeping out. When they saw the Doctors Without Borders volunteers they began crying and thanking them. At this stage, the Russian army gave the volunteers only ten minutes to leave, but they were allowed to return later with food and other support.

There have been many times while working for Doctors Without Borders when Marina has felt very frightened. One time, soldiers fired at her car and the explosion was within two metres of the wheels. Another time she was caught in the middle of a gun battle while helping to rescue civilians. Marina did not dare tell her family just how dangerous her work was. She coped with the risks by remaining calm and learning to deal with the fear.

Despite the dangers, Marina plans to continue her work with Doctors Without Borders. She feels it is necessary for the sake of the thousands of Chechen people who are still in desperate need of assistance.

Did you know?

In 2003, 89 000 refugees were living in deplorable conditions in Ingushetia with host families, in tent camps or squatting.

SALLY MURRAY Doctor

Sally Murray strongly believes in Doctors Without Borders' ideas, particularly in speaking out on health issues such as the lack of essential medicines in some countries.

Sally Murray is an Australian doctor working with HIV/AIDS patients in Kenya, Africa. She first became connected with Doctors Without Borders years ago when some of her friends went on missions and she did a refugee health course. Sally officially joined Doctors Without Borders in 2003.

Sally's work involves developing government plans for the care and treatment of those suffering from HIV/AIDS. Sally does not believe that there is no hope for these patients. She would like to use the knowledge and experience she has gained through her work to encourage better programs and the continued supply of free medicines.

Working with the HIV/AIDS patients has brought Sally a whirlwind of feelings. At different times she has felt happy, excited, angry, disappointed, inspired and frustrated. It is the stories, smiles and bravery of the thousands of patients currently being treated that keep her going.

Did you know?

In 2003, 460 people were treated with free HIV/AIDS drugs at four clinics across Kenya.

Although Sally loves her new home, she is also well aware of its harshness:

An estimated 40 million people are currently infected with HIV worldwide. Ninety-five per cent of them live in **developing countries**.

'Everything is "more" here: the dust is dustier, the clouds more bulbous and pregnant with rain, the smells dense and pungent, the putrid smoke from battered trucks and cars increasingly unbearable on the seriously dreadful roads. The little blue wooden boxes masquerading as shops with wares displayed in their wire windows about two feet square; the people walking, everywhere; the contented children playing with metal wheel frames, pushing them along with a stick; the goats, cattle, chickens and pigs wandering among the maize, ditches and roads.

Africa is so very in your face and I love it. Life is harsh though and I wouldn't usually see people die on the side of the road in lonely poverty. Or 16-year-old orphans die in hospital of tuberculosis—brave, resolute and very alone. I find it very confronting and challenging in the face of my own comfort and relative wealth.'

Sally doesn't see the point in feeling guilty, though. Instead, she encourages people to go out and do something—donate money, learn about the world's problems, help someone in trouble. She believes that if everyone shares the global work, something positive can really happen.

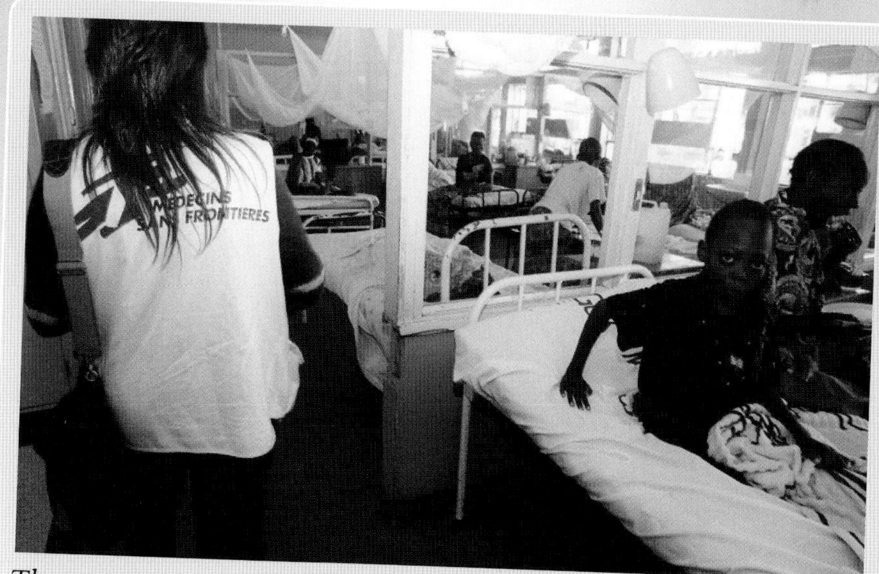

These patients, at a Doctors Without Borders clinic, are receiving free drugs to reduce the effects of HIV.

Glossary word

developing countries countries that are not yet able to provide a good standard of living for their citizens in such areas as health, education and housing

JANET KOMBA Midwife

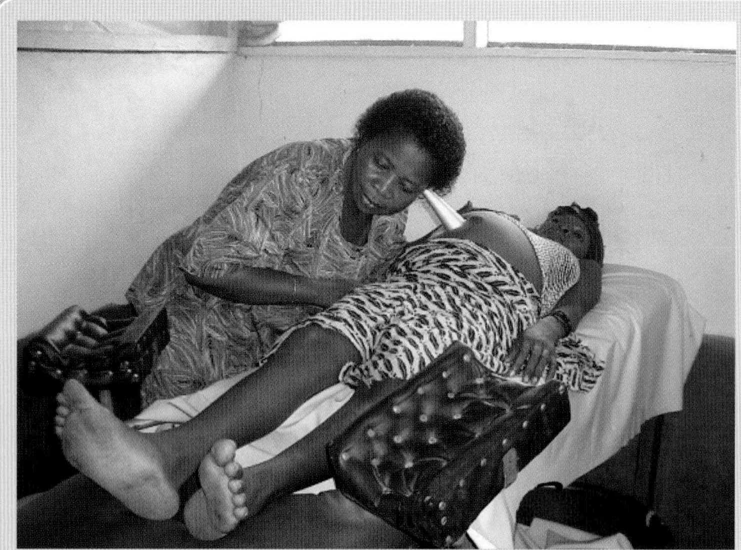

Janet Komba cares for mothers and their babies before and after their births.

Janet Komba joined Doctors Without Borders in 2003 to work as a midwife. She works in Sierra Leone, a country that has suffered severely from war for more than ten years. Many people in Sierra Leone are too poor to pay for any health care. Janet was keen to use her skills to help the people in need. By working with Doctors Without Borders, Janet can care for these sorts of people. She helps to deliver babies and provides health education, which includes hygiene and nutrition.

Much of Janet's work has been at a clinic in Tobanda refugee camp. To help the local women learn about health care, she would make up songs about healthy food and keeping things clean, and teach the songs to her patients. Singing and dancing the songs was fun for the women and made it easier for them to remember what to do.

Women were also encouraged to come to the clinic to have their babies delivered, so they could be well cared for and sent on to hospital if any problems developed.

There are only seven doctors for every 100 000 people in Sierra Leone. Life expectancy for women there is only 42 years.

Janet has learned a lot from her work with Doctors Without Borders, but she has also given up a lot. Her own children live in the capital city, Freetown, where it is safer, while she lives at the refugee camp. She can only visit them once a month. They understand that her work is important, and that if she didn't work there would not be enough money for them to go to school.

Janet enjoys delivering babies and is glad to be able to educate mothers. In some groups, people believed that certain native herbs given to babies would stop them getting stomach cramps. These herbs are actually poisonous and can kill the children. Explaining how dangerous the herbs are can save lives and is an example of how important Janet's work is.

Janet saves more lives by also being able to visit the women at home. She helps with advice on breastfeeding and encourages them to have their babies vaccinated against common diseases.

Did you know?

More than two million people were forced to leave their homes during the war in Sierra Leone. They went to live in refugee camps or neighbouring countries. Many are still there.

Women and children wait for their turn to see Janet at the clinic.

HENRY DEBUSSMAN Logistician

Henry Debussman works as a logistician for Doctors Without Borders.

Henry Debussman, from the United States of America, was looking for a job where every day was different and he could take on big challenges. He wanted to use his hands as well as his brain, and to work outdoors. Most of all he wanted his work to improve basic quality of life in places where people were desperately in need. He found all of these things when he joined Doctors Without Borders in 2002.

Henry provides the Doctors Without Borders volunteers with the tools they need to do their jobs. He helps to set up hospitals, and finds the workers places to sleep, food to eat, medicines, cars and radios to use. Henry's day is filled with buying, building and fixing things.

Doctors Without Borders has developed their own pre-packaged disaster kits, which make some of Henry's work much easier. The kits are stored at various locations and can be ready for transport within hours. They include a complete surgical theatre the size of a small conference table, and a childbirthing kit the size of a two-drawer filing cabinet. These kits are used as models by emergency relief organisations all around the world.

Because Henry's work is not normally with patients, he particularly remembers the times when he has been able to help them directly. He once helped carry an old man, who had been stuck in his bed for years, to hospital on a stretcher. Henry learned that the man's elderly wife volunteered in a local Red Cross soup kitchen, even though she already cared for her husband at home.

Did you know?

Doctors Without Borders logistical centres buy, test and store equipment including vehicles, communications materials, power supplies, water-processing facilities and nutritional supplements.

This logistician is organising for plastic sheeting to be placed over damaged roofs in the village of Corire, in Peru. It will at least provide temporary shelter over the beds inside.

Henry would like to encourage people all over the world to get personally involved, as he is, and help people in need. Henry finds his work life-changing and very fulfilling, and would like others to have the same sorts of experiences. He believes that being able to share these sorts of relationships with people from other countries builds trust and breaks down fear of different cultures.

There are many things that skilled workers can do to help in developing countries, even though that is much harder than donating money. Henry says that seeing the impact even a little help has on the disadvantaged makes up for all the stress involved.

An average Doctors Without Borders field project team has from 4 to 12 volunteers from other countries. They supervise and provide training, and work with up to 200 local staff members who teach them about the culture and needs of the community.

What can you do?

Doctors Without Borders is an agency that sends medical and support staff to dangerous situations all over the world. Although volunteers must be adult to work in the field, there are still many ways that young people can become involved.

Keep yourself informed

No matter what age you are, you can keep yourself informed about the world, so that you can make good decisions about how to help others. If you think you might like to do some sort of humanitarian work in the future, you may need to consider what subjects you choose at secondary school. Some branches can provide material and speakers to inform students about the work of Doctors Without Borders. In the United States of America, a school kit is available with lesson plans for teachers.

Fundraising activities

Some schools organise activities to raise money to help support the work Doctors Without Borders does. You may like to contact your local branch of Doctors Without Borders for ideas and advice about other ways you can help.

Doctors Without Borders aid worker Arjan Erkel was kidnapped in Chechnya in 2000. Rallies such as these were held all over the world, calling on Russian authorities to find and release him. He was released in 2004.

Glossary

cholera	infectious and often fatal diarrhoea, spread by poor sanitation
civil war	war between different groups within a country
compensation	money paid for injury or suffering
developing countries	countries that are not yet able to provide a good standard of living for their citizens in such areas as health, education and housing
disadvantaged	having a difficulty in some area, such as health, income or education, which prevents the person from leading a full life
discrimination	unfair treatment because of race, religion or other unjust reason
dysentery	a disease where the intestine becomes inflamed, which causes diarrhoea
epidemics	diseases that spread rapidly throughout a community
ethics	personal rules and standards of behaviour
famines	times when food is extremely scarce and people are starving
HIV/AIDS	a virus that stops the body from fighting against infections
human rights	a set of rights, such as the right to a fair trial, laid down by the United Nations
humanitarian	devoted to people's welfare and the promotion of social reform
logistics	organisation of people, equipment and procedures to get a job done
malaria	a fever spread by mosquitoes
neutral	not taking either side in an argument or fight
sanitation	drainage and disposal of sewage
trauma	emotional shock
tuberculosis	an infectious disease where lumps form in parts of the body such as the lungs and bones, and cause those parts to break down
underdeveloped countries	countries that are not able to provide a good standard of living for their citizens in such areas as health, education and housing
United Nations	an organisation made up of representatives from many countries, which deals with international peace and security
vaccination	medicine given to protect against infectious diseases
volunteers	people who donate their time to a cause

Index

C
cholera 14, 18, 19, 20
civil war 6, 21
civilians 6, 13, 17, 21, 23
core values 10

D
disease prevention 18–19
donations 4, 7, 11, 25, 29, 30
dysentery 20

E
emergency medical aid 5, 7, 8, 11, 12–13, 15, 18, 28
epidemics 5, 9, 13, 14, 18–19, 20
ethics 10

F
famine 5, 13, 14
feeding centres 5, 13, 14

H
health education 20–21, 26–7
history 6–9, 13
HIV/AIDS 11, 13, 21, 24–5
human rights 4

I
independence 8, 11, 16

L
local training 5, 20, 29
locations 12–13
logistics 7, 11, 14–15, 28–9
long-term projects 5, 11, 15, 16, 20–21

M
malaria 18, 19, 21
mental health 16, 17
midwifery 20, 26–7
mobile hospitals 14, 16, 17, 18, 28

N
natural disasters 5, 8, 9, 10, 11, 13, 14–15
neutrality 10, 16

R
Red Cross 6, 29
refugee camps 7, 13, 17, 22–3, 26–7

S
sanitation 5, 9, 14, 19, 20
speaking out 6, 7, 11, 24
surveillance programs 15

T
timeline 13
tuberculosis 11, 21, 25
typhoid 9

V
vaccination 14, 19, 27
volunteers 5, 7, 8, 10, 16, 17, 20, 22–9, 30

W
war casualties 5, 6, 7, 13, 16–17, 22–3, 27
water 5, 9, 13, 14, 15, 19, 20